Thanks from the Heart

compiled by
Mark Ortman

0 43422 69550 8

Cover Illustration by Kathy Davis
Cover Design by Roy Honegger

Published by Great Quotations Publishing Co.,
Glendale Heights, IL

Library of Congress Catalog Card Number: 95-81333

ISBN 1-56245-237-1

Printed in Hong Kong

To all my teachers to whom I am eternally grateful.

ap·pre·ci·a·tion *n.*

The act of estimating the qualities of people and things.

No person was ever honored for what he received;
honor has been the reward for what he has given.

— *Calvin Coolidge*

$\mathbf{W}$ho does not thank for little will not thank for much.

— *Estonian Proverb*

There is one word which may serve as a rule of practice
for all one's life — reciprocity.

— *Confucius*

Happiness is a by-product of an effort
to make someone else happy.

— Gretta Palmer

I would rather be able to appreciate things
I cannot have than to have things
I am not able to appreciate.

— Elbert Hubbard

Man lives more by affirmation than by bread.

— *Victor Hugo*

Three-fourths of the people you will ever meet are
hungering and thirsting for appreciation.
Give it to them and they will love you.

— *Dale Carnegie*

One of the deepest secrets of life is that all that is really worth doing is what we do for others.

— *Lewis Carroll*

Appreciation is the heart's memory.

Wise men appreciate all men,
for they see the good in each and
know how hard it is to make anything good.

${A}$ppreciative words are the most powerful force for good on earth.

George W. Crane

The best and most beautiful things in the world
cannot be seen, nor touched...
but are felt in the heart.

— Helen Keller

Treasure the love you receive above all.
It will survive long after your gold
and good health have vanished.

— *Og Mandino*

We make a living by what we get,
but we make a life by what we give.

com·pli·ment, *n.*

1. An expression of praise, admiration, or congratulation.
2. A formal act of civility, courtesy, or respect.

Some folks pay a compliment like they went
down in their pocket for it.

— *Kin Hubbard*

A compliment is a little touch of love
surrounded by a great imagination.

Emile Taquet

Look for strength in people, not weakness;
good, not evil.
Most of us find what we search for.

$\mathbf{Y}$ou do have the right to be generous. If he has the spirit of true generosity, a pauper can give like a prince.

— *Corrine V. Wells*

There is nothing you can say in answer to a compliment.
I have been complimented myself a great many
times, and they always embarrass me.
I always feel like they have not said enough.

— *Mark Twain*

I can live for two months on a good compliment.

Mark Twain

Some fellows pay a compliment like
they expected a receipt.

Kin Hubbard

A liar is not hard to believe when he
says nice things about you.

Most of us can run pretty well all day
on one good compliment.

If you can't get a compliment any other way,
pay yourself one.

Mark Twain

Compliments cost nothing,
yet many pay dear for them.

— German Proverb

A compliment is something like a kiss
through a veil.

— *Victor Hugo*

To say a compliment well is a high art
and few possess it.

— *Mark Twain*

Ah, now-a-days we are all of us so hard up,
that the only pleasant things to pay are compliments.
They're the only things we *can* pay.

— *Oscar Wilde*

May you always find new roads to travel;
new horizons to explore;
new dreams to call your own.

en·cour·age·ment, *n.*

To inspire to continue on a chosen course; impart
courage or confidence to; embolden; hearten.

All we can ever do in the way of good to people
is to encourage them to do good for themselves.

— *Randolph Bourne*

To teach a man how he may learn
to grow independently,
and for himself, is perhaps the
greatest service that one man can do for another.

— *Benjamin Jowett*

If you call a thing bad you do little;
if you call a thing good you do much.

— *Goethe*

The best way to help people to overcome their weak points is to do what you can to encourage and develop their strong points.

W̲e have enough people who tell it like it is —
now we could use a few who tell it like it can be.

— Robert Orben

He that does good to another does good also to
himself.

— *Seneca*

If you treat an individual as if he were what he
ought to be and could be,
he will become what he ought to be and could be.

— *Goethe*

The best way to cheer yourself up is to try
to cheer someone else up.

— Mark Twain

When someone does something, applaud!
That will make two people happy.

— Samuel Goldwyn

If you have some respect for people as they are,
you can be more effective in helping
them to become better than they are.

Everyone must row with the oars he has.

— *English Proverb*

Never discourage anyone who
continually makes progress,
no matter how slow.

— *Plato*

Tell a man he is brave,
and you help him become so.

— *Thomas Carlyle*

The best way to knock a chip off your neighbor's shoulder is to pat him on the back.

Good words cost nothing,
but are worth much.

If someone were to pay you ten cents for every kind word you ever spoke and collect five cents for every unkind word, would you be rich or poor?

A bit of fragrance always clings to the
hand that gives you roses.

— *Proverb*

A word of encouragement during failure
is worth more than
a dictionary of praise after success.

You can't help a man uphill without getting
closer to the top yourself.

— *Proverb*

Encourage all sincere attempts at achievement,
no matter how modest;
for sometimes great achievements start
from modest beginnings.

Some succeed because they are destined to,
but most succeed because they are determined to.

The first great gift we can bestow on
others is a good example.

— Morrell

$\rm E$very charitable act is a stepping stone
toward heaven.

— Henry Ward Beecher

The glory is not in never failing,
but in rising every time you fall.

— Chinese Proverb

Hope sees the invisible,
feels the intangible
and achieves the impossible.

People rarely succeed at anything
unless they have fun doing it.

I cannot change yesterday.
I can only make the most of today,
and look with hope toward tomorrow.

It is never too late to be
what you might have become.

— *George Eliot*

Inch by inch
Life's a cinch.

Yard by yard
Life is hard.

Faith is the daring of the should
to go farther than it can see.

God gives every bird its food
but does not always drop it into the nest.

— Danish Proverb

flat·ter·y, *n.*

Any exaggerated compliment or attention.

Flattery rarely hurts a man unless he inhales.

What really flatters a man is that you think
him worth flattering.

— *George Bernard Shaw*

Flattery is like chewing gum . . .
enjoy it briefly,
but don't swallow it.

Be advised that all flatterers live at the expense of those
who listen to them.

— *Jean de La Fontaine*

Many men know how to flatter,
few men know how to praise.

— *Greek Proverb*

Flattery is like counterfeit money which,
but for vanity, would have no circulation.

— *La Rouchefoucauld*

The best way to flatter a man is to tell him he's the kind of person who can't be flattered.

A flatterer is one who says things to your face
that he wouldn't say behind your back.

Flattery is a form of soft soap,
and soft soap is mostly made of lye.

— *Evan Esar*

He that flatters you more than you desire
either has deceived you
or wishes to deceive you.

— Italian Proverb

Mountains of gold would not seduce some men,
yet flattery would break them down.

Henry Ward Beecher

Flattery is a juggler,
and no kin to sincerity.

— *Sir Thomas Browne*

Some indeed there are who profess
to despise all flattery,
but even these are nevertheless to be flattered,
by being told that they do despise it.

— *Charles Caleb Colton*

If a man is vain, flatter.
If timid, flatter.
If boastful, flatter.
In all history, too much flattery
never lost a gentleman.

— Kathryn Cravens

We love flattery, even though
we are not deceived by it,
because it shows that we are
of importance enough to be courted.

— Emerson

D on't give me any honey
and spare me the sting.

— *Yiddish Proverb*

grat·i·tude, *n.*

An appreciative awareness and thankfulness,
as for kindness shown or something received.

No longer forward nor behind
I look in hope or fear;
But, grateful, take the good I find,
The best of now and here.

— *John Greenleaf Whittier*

Gratitude is a nice touch of beauty added
last of all to the countenance,
giving a classic beauty,
an angelic loveliness,
to the character.

— *Theodore Parker*

One can never pay in gratitude;
one can only pay "in kind"
somewhere else in life.

— Anne Morrow Lindbergh

Gratitude takes three forms:
A feeling in the heart,
an expression in words,
and a giving in return.

No man is so tall that he
never need stretch and
none so small that he never need stoop.

— *Danish Proverb*

He enjoys much who is thankful for little;
a grateful mind is both
a great and happy mind.

— *Thomas Secker*

Gratitude preserves old friendships,
and procures new.

When I find a great deal of
gratitude in a poor man,
I take it for granted there would be
as much generosity if he were rich.

— *Alexander Pope*

I would maintain that thanks are the
highest form of thought;
and that gratitude is
happiness doubled by wonder.

— *G. K. Chesterton*

There are two kinds of gratitude:
The sudden kind we feel for what we take,
The larger kind we feel for what we give.

— *Edwin Robinson*

Some people are always grumbling
because roses have thorns;
I am thankful that thorns have roses.

Gratitude is the most exquisite form of courtesy.

— *Jacques Maritain*

W hen I'm not thanked at all,
I'm thanked enough,
I've done my duty, and I've done no more.

— Henry Fielding

He who gives to me teaches me to give.

— *Danish Proverb*

kind·ness, *n.*

1. The quality or state of being kind.

2. An instance of kind behavior.

Always be a little kinder than necessary.

— James M. Barrie

Remember, you show courtesy to others
not because they are gentlemen,
but because you are one.

Kindness . . . loving people more than they deserve.

— Joseph Joubert

Do not ask me to be kind;
just ask me to act as though I were.

The unfortunate need people who
will be kind to them;
the prosperous need people to be kind to.

— *Aristotle*

Be kind; everyone you meet is fighting a hard battle.

— John Watson

. . . for it is in giving that we receive.

— *St. Francis of Assisi*

The greatest pleasure I know is
to do a kind deed by stealth
and have it found by accident.

— *Charles Lamb*

We cannot always oblige,
but we can speak obligingly.

— *Voltaire*

Let us be kinder to one another.

— Aldous Huxley's last words

He was so kind, he would have held
an umbrella over a duck
in a shower of rain.

— Douglas Jerrold

You can get more with a kind word and a gun
than with just a kind word.

— *Johnny Carson*

All doors open to courtesy.

— *Thomas Fuller*

Kindness in words creates confidence.
Kindness in thinking creates profoundness.
Kindness in giving creates love.

— Lao-Tzu

We hate the kindness which we don't understand.

— *Henry David Thoreau*

If you are naturally kind, you attract a lot of people you don't like.

— *William Feather*

In human relations kindness and lies are
worth a thousand truths.

— *Graham Greene*

A kind word is like a spring day.

— *Russian Proverb*

A kind word to one in trouble is often like a
switch in a railroad track . . .
an inch between wreck and smooth sailing.

— *Henry Ward Beecher*

A lot of people think that if they are kind,
somebody will take advantage of them,
and sometimes they are right.

— Don Herold

People are the kindest to those they deceive.
Thus good and evil balance.

— *Ben Hecht*

Forgiveness is a way we can alter the past.

— David Bella

Good words cost no more than bad.

— *Thomas Fuller*

The most precious thing anyone, man or business,
anybody or anything, can have is
the goodwill of others.

— *Anne Parish*

Kindness in words creates confidence.
Kindness in thinking creates profoundness.
Kindness in giving creates love.

— *Lao-Tse*

I expect to pass through life but once.
If therefore, there be any kindness I can show,
or any good thing I can do to any fellow being,
let me do it now, and not defer or neglect it,
as I shall not pass this way again.

— *William Penn*

Let us open up our natures,
throw wide the doors of our hearts and
let in the sunshine of good will and kindness.

— *O. S. Marden*

Wise sayings often fall on barren ground;
but a kind word is never thrown away.

— *Sir Arthur Helps*

Life is mostly froth and bubble,
Two things stand like stone —
Kindness in another's trouble,
Courage in our own.

— Adam L. Gordon

To fall down you manage alone but
it takes friendly hands to get up.

— *Yiddish Proverb*

Kindness is the sunshine in which virtue grows.

— *Robert Ingersoll*

The kindness I have longest remembered has
been of this sort, the sort unsaid;
so far behind the speaker's lips that
almost it already lay in my heart.
It did not have far to go to be communicated.

— *Henry D. Thoreau*

So many gods, so many creeds,
So many paths that wind and wind,
While just the art of being kind
Is all the sad world needs.

— *Ella Wheeler Wilcox*

The great acts of love are done by those who are habitually performing small acts of kindness.

The whole worth of a kind deed lies in the
love that inspires it.

— *The Talmud*

It is kindness in a person not beauty,
which wins our love.

The best portion of a good man's life -
His little, nameless, unremembered acts
Of kindness and love.

— *William Wordsworth*

One of the most difficult things to
give away is kindness,
for it is usually returned.

Whoever gives a small coin to a poor man
has six blessings bestowed upon him,
but he who speaks a kind word to him
obtains eleven blessings.

— *Talmud*

You cannot do a kindness too soon,
because you never know how soon
it will be too late.

A kind heart is a fountain of gladness,
making everything in its vicinitiy
freshen into smiles.

— *Washington Irving*

The way to happiness —
Keep your heart free from hate,
your mind from worry . . .
live simply . . .
expect little . . .
Give much.

You will find as you look back upon your life that the moments when you have really lived, are the moments when you have done things in the spirit of love.

— *Henry Drummond*

Kindness is the oil that takes
the friction out of life.

The comforter's head never aches.

— *Italian Proverb*

praise, *n.*

An expression of warm approval or admiration; strong commendation.

Among the smaller duties of life,
I hardly know any one thing more important
than that of praising where praise is due.

— *Sydney Smith*

The refusal of praise is a wish
to be praised twice.

— *La Rouchefoucald*

$\mathbf{B}$e quick to praise people.
People like to praise those who praise them.

— *Bernard M. Baruch*

The sweetest sound of all is praise.

— Xenophon

He who praises another enriches himself
far more than he does the one praised.
The poorest human being has something
to give that the richest could not buy.

— George Matthew Adams

Praise does wonders for our sense of hearing.

— *Arnold H. Glasow*

A true friend is someone who says
nice things behind your back.

Get someone to blow your own horn
and the sound will carry twice as far.

— *Will Rogers*

The meanest and most contemptible kind of praise
is that which first speaks well of a man,
then qualifies it with a "but".

— *Henry Ward Beecher*

Old praise dies unless you feed it.

— *English Proverb*

Great tranquility of heart is his who cares for neither praise nor blame.

— *Thomas a'Kempis*

Some natures are too good
to be spoiled by praise.

— *Ralph Waldo Emerson*

M odesty is the only sure bait
when you angle for praise.

— *Lord Chesterfield*

Anything scarce is valuable;
praise for example.

Sincere praise reassures individuals.
It helps them neutralize doubts
they have about themselves.

Oh, how criticism undermines people's motivation,
and praise promotes achievement.

We should give as we would receive,
cheerfully, quickly, and without hesitation;
for there is no grace in a benefit
that sticks to the fingers.

— *Seneca*

The advantage of doing one's praising to
oneself is that one can lay it on so thick
and exactly in the right places.

— *Samuel Butler*

The trouble with most of us is that we would
rather be ruined by praise
than saved by criticism.

— *Norman Vincent Peale*

I much prefer a compliment, insincere or not,
to sincere criticism.

— *Plautus*

The deepest principle of Human Nature
is the craving to be appreciated.

— *William James*

Give what you have.
To someone, it may be better
than you dare think.

— *Henry Wadsworth Longfellow*

ABOUT THE AUTHOR

Mark Ortman enjoys expressing himself as a consultant, author, publisher, teacher, composer, and speaker. Since 1983, after receiving a M. A. degree in Communications from the University of Denver, he has earned seven national instructional awards coaching people in ways to refine their interpersonal skills. Through his consulting practice in Seattle, he specializes in the hiring, selection, and development of employees. Mark has self-published the book *Now That Makes Sense*, a collection of wisdom about relating to people and will soon be releasing on cassette his enchanting instrumental music. Mark's next book will be on the subject of *Change*.